Waiting on Tiptoes

An Advent Devotional

by

Diane Karchner

Waiting on Tiptoes

Copyright © 2016 Diane Karchner

ISBN 978-0-9895633-4-5 print

ISBN 978-0-9895633-5-2 ebook

Unless otherwise noted, all Bible verses are quoted from the New International Version (NIV).

~~~~~~~~~

Dedicated to my Bible Study group of young women

who inspired the writing of this devotion by their thirst

to get closer to the God who loves them.

Each one of these women gives me hope for the

next generations as they, in turn, mentor and teach

the younger women and girls in their lives.

Truly, each of these women are

a blessing to me more than I could ever be to them.

~~~~~~~~~

Welcome to the Celebration of Advent

You will find a baby wrapped in cloths and lying in a manger. ~Luke 2.12

I did not grow up celebrating Advent. Our Protestant denomination just didn't talk about it, teach about it, or even mention it. In fact, other than pretty calendars with the little pockets I saw in stores, I had no idea it existed let alone understanding what it really meant or even what was being celebrated.

My daughter's birthday is in mid-December so we didn't plan much for Christmas until after her birthday so it wouldn't distract from her celebration. The timing worked out great to follow her birthday with a 12-Days-of-Christmas event, a gift a day until Christmas.

I guess that could have been considered our 'Advent' celebration, except that it was far from what I have come to understand about Advent.

We weren't waiting for God to arrive as much as for the fat, jolly man in red. Major difference!

Over the past 5 years, I started seeking more 'reason for the season.' Each year I picked up a different devotional and have been drawn into the majesty of the 'Wait.' Each author brought me to the manger in a different way. Each showed me the complexities along with the simplicities of what God did for us from cradle to tomb to life, with themes like love, joy, peace and hope.

I have grown to understand the duality of Advent's purpose: of anticipation and of celebration. We are celebrating the arrival of the baby Jesus, of God coming into our world, showing us how to live, giving us a hope.

We are also anticipating the return of Jesus which will usher in our eternal life with Him. It is a consummate celebration of everything that makes our faith as powerful and complete as it is. God came, God died, God returned from the dead and God is coming back.

All wrapped up in this thing called Advent. Who knew?

I wrote this devotional to celebrate that awakening, the change that has occurred in me since I started doing Christmas God's way rather than the world's way. I wrote each entry attempting to capture what moves me about that baby in a manger, that king being born, that God becoming human.

I have so much more to learn. I have so much more to absorb about what this miraculous birth means to humanity, and to our eternity.

I pray that by reading this 28-day devotional you will be moved to dig deeper into your own view of Christmas; moved, not so much by *my* words, but by the God who inspired their writing.

When you open gifts this holiday, my hope is that Christ will be a conscious presence with every ribbon untied, with every box opened, with every cookie baked because of your Advent practice.

I pray that my discovery of Advent will inspire you to find your own path to Advent, to the manger, and right up to the empty tomb.

I wish you an extremely blessed and Merry Christmas!

Diane

Waiting on Tiptoes

Wear light in your heart instead of on your trees. ~Macrina Wiederkehr

The people of the Old Testament were on tiptoes waiting for the One who was to come. They anticipated, expected, hoped for, yearned for the One; the One who had been promised for generations. In Jerusalem, the 'experts' in Jewish leadership could quote the scriptures that predicted the coming of the One.

Yet when they heard the Magi's story, they did nothing to explore it themselves. There were no special envoys, or search parties sent out to seek out their king. The possibility of the One they had waited generations for might be born, and no one lifted a finger to at least take a look, to do some exploratory research.

Were they now standing flatfooted instead of on tiptoes, anticipating, expecting?

Maybe the Star was only bright in the presence of real Hope. Mary. Joseph. The shepherds. The Magi. They all saw the bright Star. For them, it was blinding, too bright to miss, a herald of hope.

In Jerusalem, perhaps that bright star was dimmed by the brightness of the city; or maybe it was outshone by worldly pursuits, the glitz and glamour, the hypocrisy, the pride, the sin.

Let those who have eyes to see, see.

Maybe today, just maybe, like those days in Jerusalem, hope gets lost in the shiny brights of Christmas. Maybe we feel holiday-happy, but are flatfooted, with no expectations beyond the unwrappings.

But there is hope. There is always hope.

The Star reappeared to the Magi as they left the city. It lit the path to the child God. Just as for them those many years ago, we can find that bright star, that tippy-toed hope, again. It's never too late.

It's never too late to re-engage, to stand up again on our tiptoes and search the skies for the Star, waiting.

Dear God, shield our eyes from the brightness of our worldly celebration so we can see the Star. Help us to find and hold tight to its hope. Teach us, again, to stand on our tippy-toes in wide-eyed anticipation of You. And, dear Lord, help us to help others find it for the first time, or even, to re-find it all over again. ~Amen

~~~~~~~~

Waiting on Tiptoes
12

The Hope in the Light

The people walking in darkness have seen a great light; on those living in the land of the shadow of death a light has dawned.
~Isaiah 9.2

Christmas is all about the birth of a baby. But in that humble stable was born so much more than an infant. God came to earth that night, and by doing that He made it ok to be human by becoming one.

Without that baby, the world had a waning hope that God would help, a feeble hope pre-Christmas that God might still be there for them. He had been there before. Many times. But after all the disobedience, all the turning away, could the world even hope for anything more than a Noah-flood-like end? Would God help them yet again?

God responded that night in the stable.

All through the Old Testament, hope was etched in between the lines, woven into God's refrain from all-out wrath. Hope had been their legacy. It was still part of their story, of our story.

We can trust in the hope that God comes through. He did. He does.

In this season of Advent, what is it that we have hope in, and for, and about? What is the heart-string hope that we hang onto in our prayers, in our daydreaming.

Where do we hang our personal hope?

For me, it's the hope that everyone I know will feel and know the love of our generous, faithful God in a real, tangible way.

My heart aches with the thought that some people live without Jesus' saving grace and love as a part of their life.

That's my hope. It makes me smile.

Hope always makes me smile.

Thank you, God, for coming through for all of us, for shining that light into our darkness and making that darkness bright and shiny. Like the tree tinsel that glows on our trees, draw us closer to the brightness of that manger once again. Our hope is in you. ~Amen

~~~~~~~~

Waiting on Tiptoes
16

Security of Hope

We have this hope as an anchor for the soul, firm and secure. ~Hebrews 6.19

If we believe...

- that God came to earth as a baby...
- that he grew up to be an adult, a human with his feet planted in the earthen soil...
- that he died for us...
- that he rose from the dead and talked and walked with his disciples
- that he ascended into heaven to reside at the right hand of God...
- that he will return...
- that our eternal future is assured...

...then there is no reason not to have hope.

Hope. It is the house built on the rock. It is the good soil of God's kingdom growth. It is the treasure we will sell everything we own to possess.

Hope is the reason to give the grace that God gave us on that Christmas morning. We need only embrace the contentment of being fully awake to that foundation of hope.

Hope as a foundation? It can be. It may already be and you have forgotten, or are unaware.

Our hope started that night in the manger, but extends way beyond. The manger is the beginning of what we can see God doing. Beyond that manger, there was—there is—so much more happening as God's entire creation groans in anticipation of His return.

Hope gives us the chance to rise above despair and fear and isolation. Hope enables us to live in joy and peace, if we just grab hold of it.

I value this hope that God has provided. I cling to it when the daily news gets ugly, when my world seems to be growing more evil by the minute. I hang on, sometimes by my fingertips, to the thought that *'God's got this'* even when my eyes and ears betray that very notion.

But still I cling. And I will never let go.

Nor will He.

Dear Lord, remind us by your Spirit's gentle encouragement, that you did, and are doing, so much more than being born in a humble manger. Help us to grab hold of the bigger picture. Let us cling to that hope that was born that night in a humble, dirty stable. For with you all things are possible. ~Amen

~~~~~~~

Waiting on Tiptoes

The Spark of Hope

Hope. It's the only thing stronger than fear. A little hope is effective. A lot of hope is dangerous. A spark is fine, as long as it's contained. ~ President Snow, *Hunger Games*

As Christians, we sparkle with the hope of the birth of our faith's centrality. It is a time to rejoice, to be glad. But there is so much more wrapped in this hope, in this celebration.

For all too many, it stops at the birth of a baby. *Unto us a child is born.*

Even as they celebrate the biggest event in the history of mankind, it's as if they received a huge gift but removed only the outer wrapping without lifting the lid to see the gift's fullness.

Rather, they embrace a glimmer of a faith that brings the possibility of eternity mingling in the tinsel and gifts and shiny brights.

They don't see beyond the manger, beyond the birth of a baby. They don't see the long awaited Savior. They don't see the Cross at Christmas.

Yet it is there.

Mary and Joseph knew that something big was going on when the angels soothed their early fears. The shepherds knew it was bigger than a spark when the angels started singing. The magi who travelled a long way knew they were pursuing more than an oddly bright star. Even Herod suspected and lashed out in violence against any that might threaten his future power.

That baby, that little child, was the uncontainable spark of hope that would become more than just dangerous.

It would change the world forever.

Dear Lord, let our eyes be wide open to the fullness of what Jesus being born into the world really means. As we celebrate with family and friends, help us to never lose sight of the magnificence of the gift that lay in that manger.

Thank you for becoming human, giving us the most incredible, unbelievable, indescribable gift ever! We never want to slow down and settle for the outer wrapping, but let our hope drive us to rip it wide open. ~Amen

~~~~~~~

Waiting on Tiptoes
24

Take Notice

Hope does not disappoint us because God has poured out his love into our hearts by the Holy Spirit whom he has given us. ~Romans 5.5

Mary was a teenager when she was pregnant with Jesus; Joseph probably not much older. They agreed to take on the shame and scorn and embarrassment of an unmarried pregnancy. For nine months they weathered whatever social stigma was attached to that shame in those days (and it was considerable!).

Perhaps having conversations with actual angels helps you get past the mean looks of your neighbors.

For three decades they raised this boy to manhood. They raised him as a Jew. They raised him in Nazareth, in obscurity. They raised him without paparazzi watching his every move.

They didn't write any books or do reality TV lauding their success in raising this special child. They were just faithful parents.

Just as with Joseph and Mary, God wants us to live for Him, to choose Him, to serve Him, to obey His commands that are meant for our good. We sometimes yearn to play a role that has significance, that will get noticed, that will be applauded and revered. We yearn to be chosen, to be plucked out of obscurity and noticed.

And maybe some of us will be. More likely, we will not.

Instead God might choose us to be steadfast and patient and filled with hope. Expectant, waiting, eager, hopeful. Loving him and living a life that screams 'hey, God is good!'

Our hope cannot lie in the things that the world sees as important—to be noticed, respected, and applauded by everyone. The hope of that will lead us to a world of empty.

Our hope has to start and end where Mary's did. She treasured and pondered all the things that God was doing around her (Luke 2.19). She took notice, but did not seek to be noticed.

Dear Lord, help us to notice all the little things you are drenching us with. Teach us to treasure and ponder them in our hearts as Mary did, every day, not just in this season of celebration. Help us to absorb the huge idea that we are special to you no matter who notices or applauds. Teach us, Lord, through your Spirit, to enjoy every minute, to be hopeful in every second, knowing that the hope we have in you will never disappoint. ~Amen

~~~~~~~~

Waiting on Tiptoes
28

The Waiting Room

See, I am doing a new thing! Now it springs up; do you not perceive it? I am making a way in the desert and streams in the waste-land. ~Isaiah 43.19

Advent is a season of waiting.

We humans don't wait well. We are not natural wait-ers. We like to move, to make progress, to keep things going. Waiting is inactive, immobile. It takes much too much patience for this waiting thing!

At the very heart of the Advent season is the understanding that what we await, what we hope for, has already begun. It is already in motion. It has already taken steps forward and started moving along.

Without our help, Jesus is coming back for us. The wheels are already turning, and have been for centuries.

What we are waiting for is already on its way.

The waiting of Advent, the real hope of Advent, is the assurance that we are safe, that we are taken care of, that we have a home with Jesus. Forever. Without doing anything but believe.

Even with that assurance, with that hope, fear often crushes the patience that this waiting requires. We cannot just wait around, we must act. Nothing can happen without us doing something, without us getting out of the waiting room, right? God can't possibly do it all, we have to do something, right?

Perhaps, it's not the waiting that bugs us as much as the lack of control that waiting on God requires.

Perhaps it is trust, and not patience, that we need more of in this season. Trust that God will do what he says even if it's later than we think it should be.

Dear God, we are so thankful that you are upstream working on things for us, for our good, for our eternity. Help us to deeply absorb that

into our weak humanness, so that waiting be-
comes easier. Ingrain in our souls the simplicity
of the truth that you have already prepared a
way for us; a way for us right into your forever-
presence. ~Amen

~~~~~~~~

Waiting on Tiptoes
32

The Imperfect Birthing Room

The Word became flesh and made his dwelling among us. ~John 1.14

There was no room in the Inn. This teenage girl, in the throes of active labor pain, was denied more than just a room. She was denied a bed, a pail of clean water, a clean blanket, a little privacy.

But she did get a stable. A perfect stable. A perfect place for animals to live. Dirty feeding trough on one side, smelly manure covering the floor, hay crackling under foot. It was not the sweet little nativity scene that sits on our mantels each Christmas eve.

This was to become the most unlikely delivery room for the Savior of the human race, of the world. But no matter where, Jesus was to be born.

The bigger picture, God's plan, was not to be denied. Nothing could, nothing would, stop or even slow the forward momentum of our hope.

God did not wait for the kind of perfection we look for. He did not wait until a room was available, until a midwife could be rustled up somewhere in Bethlehem, for the perfect fluffy blanket to be found. Mary could have had the baby before they even started traveling. Or the baby could have been born when they arrived in Jerusalem.

Any of those ways seem more ideal to us than the dirty stable. But God moved in spite of what we see as imperfections.

God chose the stable. The star above. The hay below.

There is nothing perfect about that in our worldly eyes; yet all was perfect in God's. God showed us His humbling way to greatness. Our perfect hope lies in that imperfect manger. In that moment, in that unlikely place, God was born as one of us.

Humbling imperfection won over perfection.

Dear Lord, teach us to sit by the manger, in the dirty stable, and absorb what imperfection can produce, what can come of humble beginnings. Show us, by your birth, how to have hope without throwing our human, critical judgement all over it. Help us to know how to live a life for you, not afraid to be in humble places, doing unglamorous things, for your glory alone. ~Amen

~~~~~~~

Waiting on Tiptoes
36

Choosing Heart Peace

He will teach us his ways, so that we walk in his paths. He will judge between the nations and will settle disputes for many peoples. They will beat their swords into plowshares and their spears into pruning hooks. Nation will not take up sword against nation, nor will they train for war anymore. ~Isaiah 2.3-4

We have our own ideas of what a world at peace, a ceasing of violence across the globe, would look like. The world would 'live as one' as John Lennon wrote. Kumbaya, right?

But world peace, as we define it, would mean that billions of citizens of this globe would just decide in unison to 'give peace a chance.' And then stick to it. Each of the billions of people on earth would have a simultaneous role in such an extraordinary occurrence.

Yet in all of human existence we have never gotten close to this outside of the Garden.

Every day, we are barraged with messages that nurture our feelings of helplessness towards ever attaining that nirvana. It's a beauty of a dream. And it would be a true miracle.

But God already delivered that miracle. He already gave the world a way out. He already provided a way to peace. He already gave us the manger that led to the Cross. He gave us this perfect escape route, the only way to world peace.

But the world is a fallen place. And as much as we all want everyone to just get along, it will not happen. At least not until Jesus returns as Isaiah prophesied.

Until that true peace of God comes, things can feel pretty disheartening, especially in the days that seem drenched in evil and terror and dishonesty.

But God didn't leave us powerless, to be cut down by discouragement in these times of waiting. He gave us a spirit of power, and the free will to choose not to be timid and afraid. We get to choose peace in the one place that we can control. In our heart.

For God did not give us a spirit of timidity, but a spirit of power, of love and of self-discipline. ~2 Timothy 1.7

Dear Lord, the world seems scarier than ever, and the violence moves ever closer to our own neighborhoods. Remind us to just choose your peace rather than the headlines of fear. Thank you for never leaving us even when fear threatens to overcome us, for never turning your back on us even when peace is far from our hearts. Thank you for taking care of our world and winning in the end. ~Amen

~~~~~~~

Waiting on Tiptoes
40

The Grace of a Doily

Whatever you did for one of the least of these brothers of mine, you did for me. ~Matthew 25.40

In Kenya, I had the opportunity to visit a woman who lives in the slum. Her home was tiny—no bigger than a backyard shed—with walls and roof made of corrugated metal, a cooking fire smoldering in a hole dug in the center of the dirt floor, no electricity, no running water. Her bathroom was the gutter that ran down the center of her dirt street.

As I greeted her, she motioned for me to have a seat on the dilapidated, discolored, "cushioned" chair in the corner. I gently lowered myself onto the chair, sinking nearly to the floor. A discolored lace doily, the kind my grandmother had crocheted way back when, lay across one arm of the chair.

As I sat listening to her, asking about her life, I stroked the doily. The stitches as lovely as I had ever seen, faded pink flowers embroidered on the center. It was so out of place to me, this lacy delicacy in this hovel, in this dirty slum. Too clean, too white (dingy by western standards), to be an every day covering.

That sweet, kind Christian woman, who had so little, put out her best for me. She had no riches, no china cups in which to serve the warm chai tea, no way to make the dirt floor any cleaner. But she had a doily. A doily that she put out for me, an honored guest in her home. A kindness beyond expectation. She honored me with her very best.

It's been 7 years since I touched that doily; yet, it continues to remind me:

Of God coming to us in the guise of a stranger.

Of how Jesus honored the widow who gave what little she had.

Of the hugeness of His gift that was wrapped in dirty swaddling clothes, illuminated only by the bright star of hope.

That doily reminds me to give grace. All the time, whenever I can, at every single opportunity. Just as Jesus did.

Dear Lord, we miss so much of what you want us to see and appreciate. We miss the possibility to show grace as you did to us. Forgive us. Give us eyes that see the opportunities you give us to show kindness—to put out our special doily. And let us see the kindnesses and grace offered to us. Lord, in this season of peace, give us hearts and spirits that rest only in you. ~Amen

~~~~~~~~

Waiting on Tiptoes
44

Peaceful Acceptance

Turn from evil and do good; seek peace and pursue it. ~Psalm 34.14

In Jesus' time, women were not treated well. In fact, they were less than second class citizens. So, the fact that God even chose a woman, a virgin, to be his conduit to humanness is amazing. He could have just transported himself into the world as an adult. After all, this is God we're talking about.

Mary was a woman who loved God. In a time when women could not study with a rabbi, her knowledge was surprising. Gabriel said she was favored by God so she must have had something going on. That something—that knowledge and love for God—was revealed in her chat with Elizabeth shortly after her encounter with the angel. (Luke 1.40)

It was always a curiosity to me that Mary spent three months with Elizabeth, almost to the birth of cousin John. My guess was she needed to talk out with someone—anyone—this pregnancy.as.virgin thing; share with someone else who had a miracle of pregnancy. (And Elizabeth probably enjoyed having someone to talk to since her husband could not talk! See Luke 1.20)

But maybe, and this is a big maybe, Mary wanted to get used to the idea in solitude and meditation, away from the prying eyes of judgement at home. She might have needed some alone-time to absorb the idea that God - THE God of the universe - was inside her. Getting over the initial jubilation, the 'yippee, He picked me,' she was beginning to settle into the overpowering weight of its seriousness. She was a teenager who was asked to give birth to God as a human. What woman wouldn't need some time to think about this?

She went to Elizabeth's excited and bubbling over; she gave birth to Jesus nine months later with an attitude of thoughtfulness, pondering things in her heart in peace beyond her years.

She took the time to accept and settle into the kind of peace that only comes from God. She took the time to rest in God, and found a strength that would sustain her, that would remain with her through a life that would sting of tragedy and loss, and of unbelievable joy.

Dear Lord, help us to go beyond the surface of religion and dig into the reality of the peace that comes from accepting how ferociously you love us. Remind us, through your Spirit, to pray as if we believed completely, beyond what we see, beyond what we feel. Thank you for the lessons of Mary. ~Amen

~~~~~~~

Waiting on Tiptoes
48

Top of the Stairs

Those who hope in the Lord will renew their strength; they will soar on wings like eagles; they will run and not grow weary, they will walk and not be faint. ~Isaiah 40.31

When our kids were young, Christmas Day was a big event, as it is for every little Santa-believer. Christmas morning came especially early, at least for them, and by default, for us. They ran into our bedroom at dawn, knowing the rule of not venturing downstairs without us. We insisted on 'paving the way' to the entrance into their Santa world.

Truth be told, we weren't paving anything for them. We had done that the night before, often into the wee hours of the morning depending on how many pieces Santa left for us to assemble into some gadget, or riding thing. Rather, we wanted to make coffee, put some bread in the toaster, turn on the tree lights. All to create a calmness for us, the weary adults, as we watched and enjoyed the pandemonium that was about to break loose.

On the steps above our head was the chatter of two little voices. Nervous anticipation, bathed in the hope of their hearts' desires being fulfilled just moments away. Their voices cried out every thirty seconds or so.

"Just a couple more minutes. Be patient." Toast wasn't buttered yet, coffee was still brewing.

Although it may not feel it at the time, hopeful anticipation is usually laced with joy. As nerve-wracking and nail-biting as it may seem in the moment, it will eventually be looked back on as one of the high points of life. Today, our adult kids smile when they tell of the times they peeked, of the many steps they tiptoed down when we were busy about our calm-creating activities. They would peek, and the peek would give them even more hopeful anticipation.

Jesus has told us that He is coming back. He has given us a peek, by the presence of the

Holy Spirit in us, of what our eternity will be like. We have tiptoed down the steps and peeked into the manger to see what was coming. We sit at the top of the steps, even as we celebrate what already took place on that starry night, and we rest in the anticipation of the greatest hope that humankind has ever known.

Dear Lord, sometimes we *just can't wait* for you to come back. We get overwhelmed and snowed under with the fears of this world, with the doubt and worry that sometimes threatens to consume us. But yet, when we remember to sit at the top of the steps waiting for the unwrapping, for the final arrival, our hope is renewed. Thank you for giving us the Holy Spirit to remind us time and time again that you are real and here and on the way. ~Amen

~~~~~~~

Trusting in Peace

The shipwrecked don't seek peace, because by living they have it. ~Brennan Manning

People are running after peace all the time. Peace on earth. Peace in their family. Peace at work. Peace in their heart.

In our state of constant busy-ness we can't seem to find a lick of rest, of solitude, of peace. We are constantly running after the elusive, never stopping to consider that we already have it.

When Jesus spoke of sending the Holy Spirit, he said that we will have something the world won't be able to give us.

Peace I leave with you; my peace I give you. I do not give as the world gives. Do not let your heart be troubled and do not be afraid.
~John 14.27

We already have it so we don't have to keep seeking it.

We can look and seek and turn over every rock looking for it but only God coming to earth made this kind of peace possible.

Sit still in this moment to absorb the enormity of this. The peace of God—not of humans, not of Oprah, not of karma, not of anything we can imagine—is ours. It is *already* ours.

His peace—the one described in the Creation story as rest—is one of stillness, of knowing that all is well, of work completed, of faith well-lived. His peace is more than a calmness. It is life-giving and joy-enhancing.

His birth made this new thing possible, this thing called peaceful living.

We can, in all our human wisdom, hang on to our own ways of finding peace. The ones that are fleeting and shallow.

Or, we can choose His way to peace, the one that is deep and whole and never-ending.

Our choice. It is there for the taking.

Dear God, thank you for coming to earth, for living as we do, understanding our struggle for peace in our hearts. Thank you for giving us the peace that you understand so completely because you lived as one of us. Help us to remember it is already ours. Help us to celebrate this in our heart, showing a world struggling to find it what real peace looks like. ~Amen

~~~~~~~

Waiting on Tiptoes
56

The Angels Sang to Them

As for me, it is good to be near God. ~Psalm 73.28

If I could be any character in the Christmas story, I would be a shepherd. They lived in the fields, literally, with their sheep. Ok, not a glamorous profession. Other than Christmas night I am not sure their career path had much future or respect. But still...

There they were, on the side of a hill, tending their herd, minding their own business. Suddenly, an Angel appears (an Angel!). And the light, it was so bright that fear filled their entire bodies. The Angel said not to be afraid (the Angel talked!), so they weren't.

Then a 'great company of the heavenly host' (how many is that!?) sang to them. In unison. *Glory to God* is right. How could you not? This was beyond a fuzzy dream or vision! The gates of heavens opened up and its inhabitants filled the sky. For goodness sake! The magi can have the one really bright star, I'll take the heavenly host any time!

Then the Angels left them and went back to heaven. Say, what? Did a door open and they filed through it? Did the clouds engulf them in a heavenly transport?

We run our eyes over these words and don't grasp the magnificence of it. We miss the exuberant celebration that was happening when God came to earth. The Angels were super-excited! They left heaven to sing about it!

Then, the story goes, the shepherds got to the stable. Hmmmm, just a baby with a teen mom, and a dad who looked tired. Yet, the Angels came out of heaven to tell about this little one. There was something to this, something magnificent, beyond their pay grade to really grasp.

What peace must have flooded their hearts as they returned to their flock. The long awaited Savior had been born, and they got to see him, to tell of him. These low class, smelly loners; these keepers of the flocks.

It must have been an incredible night.

Dear God, open our hearts to see the details of that night. Help us not to gloss over them, just reciting the words, ignoring the majesty of the moment. Help us to resist the temptation to move too quickly to the shiny tree, to the ribbons and bows, but to dwell in the awe of God's arrival on earth, to celebrate it, just as the heavenly host did that starry night. ~Amen

~~~~~~~~

Waiting on Tiptoes
60

Peace in the In-Between

Comfort, comfort, my people, says your God.
~Isaiah 40.1

We spend a lot of time trying to get comfortable. The right shoes, the right mattress, the right temperature in the room. All so we can have a level of contentment, alleviation of discomfort and unknowing.

The truth be told, we don't like the uncertainty of discomfort.

We like clarity. When we don't have it, we tend to detour off the road seeking something to make it less uncomfortable. We make up answers, seeking a way to comfort, or we ignore the things that we can't make any sense out of —at least what doesn't make much sense to our human minds.

As we are caught up in this season of celebration, we don't want to think too much about what it really means—this birth of a kid who eventually walks on water.

We don't want to think about the weirdness of it all, about the stuff that doesn't make any sense. We don't want to get too deep because we don't have all the answers and that is just way too uncomfortable.

But God doesn't care if we get all that He is doing. He doesn't care if we, in our humanness, understand the bigger picture. He just wants us to trust him. By doing that it clears out any uncomfortableness, if we let it.

God wants us to get comfortable in the in-between, in the paradoxes that may never be clear. He wants us to trust that He's got it all under control. He wants us to be cozy-comfortable in Him even when the world seems to be coming apart at the seams, when clarity seems hard to grab hold of.

He came so He could stay. He was born so He could die. He left so He could return. It is the grand paradox: the amazing, confusing willingness of a God who is just too big, too powerful, too loving for our little human brains and hearts to absorb.

Trusting in Him, allows us to be comfortable to wait in this in-between place. We need not be uncomfortable, nor do we need to wait alone.

We wait with Him.

Not a bad companion to have in the waiting room.

Dear God, here we are, the impatient. Here we are in this in-between waiting time. Help us, when we get itchy uncomfortable, to stay the course. Give us wisdom to accept that we will never have all the answers to the things that are too big for us to ever understand. Help us to trust you more and more with uncomfortable questions and doubt and confusion. Give us the gift of your comfort and peace in spite of our human need for answers. ~Amen

~~~~~~~

The Joy of Anticipation

But his mother treasured all these things in her heart. And Jesus grew in wisdom and favor with God and men. ~Luke 2.51-52

Mary was visited by Gabriel, who told of her upcoming pregnancy, of the child she would soon have. She knew that this was a divine event. Joseph knew that. Elizabeth knew that. But few others did. This divine interruption in the trajectory of an evil world was not celebrated as it should have been.

Elizabeth, her cousin, celebrated her own pregnancy, thankful to God for 'taking away her disgrace among the people.' A son born to a once-barren woman was not a little thing. It was party-worthy! (Luke 1.25)

The Bible says that the community shared Elizabeth's joy. They were thrilled for her. John was born to great celebration, probably surrounded with midwives and prayer and dancing. (Luke 1.58)

Not so for Mary.

She was pregnant before she was married. She was very young. She was away from home, giving birth to her first child in a dirty stable. There is not much in the Bible about how Mary and Joseph got by during her pregnancy, their time of shame. After Jesus' birth, they did 'vacation' in Egypt for awhile. Maybe that helped, a reprieve from the judgmental looks and gossipy words. They did eventually have other children. Maybe that helped the family to be more accepted in the community.

But no matter the beginning of his life in this world, it was said of Jesus as a young boy that 'he grew in wisdom and stature, and in favor with God and men.' From the little the Bible tells us about Jesus as a boy, he seemed like a gifted kid growing up in a normal family, who happened to be able to hold his own in a synagogue with the experts of the Law at the age of 12.

'His mother treasured all these things in her heart.' She knew there would be more. She knew that God had plans for her smart son. Plans that were bigger than being a carpenter in Nazareth, bigger than being the oldest brother, or the smartest kid on the block.

Mary started in faith, and spent her life pondering it, probably focused on the last words that the angel Gabriel said to her years before. 'Nothing is impossible with God.'

She pondered the possibilities of God. Can we do any less with our lives?

Dear God, show us how to expand the horizons of our possibilities. For if you are the God of the impossible, then our view is much too limited. Give us courage whenever we draw the boundaries of possibilities to what we can see, what we can imagine in our own strength. Thank you that you have given us your strength and your power through the Holy Spirit to accomplish whatever you would have us do for you. ~Amen

~~~~~~~

Waiting on Tiptoes
68

Refreshing Our Gift Giving

Thanks be to God for his indescribable gift!
~2 Corinthians 9.15

Christmas is about gifts. It is. We'd all like to say that this holiday is only about the baby in a manger but in our culture He is so often an after thought, a Christmas Eve church event on the long list of holiday events.

In our passion 'to do it right' we have rules around our giving. If someone gifts, you must gift back. If a gift is small, you gift back small. If large, gift back large. And then it gets funky. If you think someone will gift large, you gift large first. If you think they will cheap-out, cheap it down.

The escalation, expectation and perverseness of this could be endless. It can be a nasty business, this human gift-giving.

Yet that is far from what the gift of the baby in the manger was all about.

God's giving carries with it the sheer and complete impossibility of an equal payback gift. God's giving of a gift this large, this magnificent, finds us with no way to reciprocate. We can only refuse or accept. No in-betweens.

Instead, we are left in gratitude-mode; to wallow in it, or rejoice because of it. For the wallowers, it leaves their hearts in an asthmatic cramp. They want to escape the uncomfortableness of owing another, constantly in turmoil to do, be, act right in order to be deserving of it before they decide to actually embrace it.

But for those who accept and fully embrace this gift, it is like having air forced through their lungs in a wave of refreshment.

It is a full acceptance of the impossibility of a payback, that there is nothing we can do that is big enough, expensive enough, equal enough.

With God's gift, there is none of the shame, no unworthiness, no guilt that human gift-giving carries with it.

God wants us, with His free giving, to rest from all that crap. He wants us to 'stop striving, and know that I am God' (Psalm 46.10 NASB) and accept that what He gives has no strings attached. There is no chance to reciprocate because there is nothing that could compare, and no way we could earn or deserve it.

He just wanted to give it, free of charge. And He wants us to choose to just accept it.

Dear God, thank you for being our resting place. Thank you for giving us the peacefulness of non-reciprocation. Help us, in our own giving, to attach no strings of expectations to the ribbons and bows. Teach us to give so freely, so purely, that others will feel fresh air rush into their hearts as they open the box. Thank you for this season that reminds us how to gift like you do. ~Amen

~~~~~~~

Waiting on Tiptoes
72

Joy Beyond Happy

But the angel said to them, "Do not be afraid. I bring you good news of great joy that will be for all the people." ~Luke 2.10

Depending on the translation, the Bible uses the words "happy" and "happiness" about 30 times, while "joy" and "rejoice" appear over 300 times.

We all know 'happy' by its warm, fuzzy feeling, by the sound of its laughter, its spirit of frivolity. It is a good feeling, this 'happy' state. But it is fleeting, shallow in its ability to stay the course, to last past the initiating event.

Happiness depends on things outside ourselves, things that happen to us, around us.

Although the two are often used interchangeably, joy and happiness are miles apart in true worth. Unlike happiness, joy depends on the humbling acceptance of God's plan. Joy knows without a doubt who controls our beginning and our end.

Joy isn't giggly madness. It is God-grounded optimism.

Joy permeates a life. Even in the wake of profound sadness, tragedy and disappointment. Joy does not fail. It is knowing—even if it seems only a flicker of flame in the hard times —that God will come through. Somehow, in some way. God will show up.

Joy, the heavy lifting side of happy, carries a willingness to wait, the anticipation of good in the face of humanly impossible odds. It is not something that we can muster up on our own. It is not a choice to be joyful, as much as it is a choice to be His. Joy comes when you seek God.

The news that the angels announced was beyond just a good news story on a starry night. It was a story that would have long lasting effect on 'all of the people.' It wasn't just a fleeting moment of giggles and laughter. It was a deep knowing of good things.

When you seek Him, truly and deeply, joy flows. There is no way to stop it.

Dear God, we stand humbled by your love. A love so great that you gave us the ability to sit quietly in joy, no matter what the world is throwing at us. Help us to seek you first, before everything else. Transform us into a people of joy, standing out in a world of fleeting, happy feelings. Let our lives of joy show the world what is possible with God. ~Amen

~~~~~~~~

Waiting on Tiptoes
76

Overtaken by Joy

Gladness and joy will overtake them, and sorrow and sighing will flee away. ~Isaiah 35.10

I like the word 'overtake' in this verse. I like it because it bears an element of surprise. Not that I like surprises because I rarely do. But this one seems to be one of those little private happenings.

You go for a walk, you are taking a warm bath, you are sitting in the sunshine. And something changes inside. We notice that we aren't worried anymore. We aren't anxious about tomorrow. Our sadness has dissipated. The negativity is somehow fled away.

When we walk with God, He does that, even though we barely notice His hand in it. Relieved of the bad vibes, we move on without much thought to it. We had it, now it's gone, and we are glad. We scoff it off with 'it must have been something I ate.'

We rarely pause to take in that moment of awareness to thank the One who overtook us, who chased the crap out of our head and our heart. We don't notice that the rest of the day became a whole lot better because of that overtaking.

The shepherds got it. Overtaken by the heavenly hosts, literally, they must have been filled with a joy that overwhelmed. So much joy had consumed them that they had to go see the reason. Immediately. They were greatly moved, keenly aware.

We are rarely even aware. But, c'mon! We don't get the heavens opening up before our eyes, so maybe awareness is more dependent on the manner of the overtaking, of what our eyes can actually see.

Or maybe not.

Perhaps our lackadaisical attitude mirrors our own lack of understanding of what really happens when we are overtaken by God. The heavens do open up. God does come here, to earth, close to us. In fact, in us.

The sorrow and sighing flee, not because of our human strengths, but because God did something. In us.

The shepherds have nothing on us! They ran to the stable, hoping it was God.

We don't have to run anywhere. We already have God 24/7.

Dear Lord, overtake us with gladness and joy any time, anywhere. Help us to be keenly aware of what you are doing in our lives, even if it's after the fact, after the sorrow and sighing have fled. Forgive us when we haven't noticed, when we take credit for the work that you are doing. Draw us close, Lord, so we can see more of you. ~Amen

~~~~~~~

Waiting on Tiptoes
80

Joy of Creation

Do not conform any longer to the patterns of this world, but be transformed by the renewing of your mind. ~Romans 12.2

A pattern: the usual way of doing things, the way it has always been done, the accepted way.

Evil is a pattern. Herod was a pattern. Roman tyranny was a pattern. A pattern of abuse and misuse of power. The way it had been for so long.

Power is a two-edged sword. When used for evil, it will crush and destroy. When used for good, it will, ironically, empower those it has power over.

We sit in that in-between place of trying to understand how people can use power in such evil ways. Child abusers. ISIS terrorists who behead and murder. Sex traffickers. Mean, abusive, evil people. All are living patterns of the misuse of power.

When the oppressiveness of evil seems so close at hand, we have to fight the pressure to conform to the worldly pattern of discouragement and negativity. We have to rise above that pattern.

God didn't come to earth so that He could become like us, to show us a better version of the worldly pattern in which we are already entrenched. He came to earth to show us a completely new pattern, a new way of life unlike the world's way. He wants us to adopt a God-powerful pattern, infused with the Holy Spirit.

In Job 38, God said that while He was creating the world 'the morning stars sang together and all the angels shouted for joy.' They sang and shouted while God was creating art, while God was forming the oceans and the air and the clouds in the sky. They sang. The stars sang! The angels cheered!

Now that's power. This is the kind of power that celebrates creation, not destruction. There is nothing on earth that can withstand that kind of power. This is the power that lives within us, that empowers us to overcome the patterns of this world.

We need not follow the world's patterns. We have a better way. And it started in a manger.

Dear God, forgive us our foolishness. Forgive us for thinking that you cannot totally annihilate evil, all of it, and that you will. Help us to be patient and in the waiting take on your pattern that resides in us; the power of the Holy Spirit that can overcome anything. ~Amen

~~~~~~~

Waiting on Tiptoes
84

Joy in Prayer

Pray continually. ~1Thessalonians 5.17

Prayer comes in handy. It makes you feel good to pray when things are tough. It just seems right to do it when emotions wash over you, or fear grips at your throat. God hears those kind of prayers.

We are down for the count and need a hand up, a chance to fight on our own for another day. *Dear God, help me get up off the floor.* And He does. Again and again, He gives peace in those desperate times.

It says something about how we are created that we so automatically and willingly turn to God in times of crisis. Maybe we instinctively know that He will willingly and graciously comfort us.

We often miss the sheer magnitude of what is happening in those moments when He meets our need.

Too bad. This is not an insignificant miss.

When we use prayer only when we are desperate, we miss the long term benefits of being close to God. Joy is one of those benefits that cannot be under-valued.

Joy. It comes from shifting from a me-focus to a God-focus. It is a deep and spiritual abiding. It's not fleeting emotion but rather gut-level comfortable, a subconscious wholeness that sticks with you.

When you have experienced it, you never forget it. You never want to lose it.

Yet we miss it when we pray only when we need a quick fix, when we seek that shot of saturated, caffeinated adrenaline. God does not want to sit on the sidelines of our life, just jumping in when you happen to think of asking Him in. Although He will.

God wants us to choose him. First. Always.

A life saturated in prayer connects us with Him on a continuously open line, so that He can give us what we don't even know we are missing. Joy.

Dear God, life isn't easy sometimes. We are so thankful that you are here with us in those hard times. Teach us to include you in the good times as well. Thank you for staying in our corner even when we ignore you. Help us to settle into a life that puts you in the center so that we can experience the joy that you want us to have. ~Amen

~~~~~~

Waiting on Tiptoes
88

Joy Always Returns

Be strong and courageous. Do not be afraid or terrified because of them, for the Lord your God goes with you; he will never leave you nor forsake you. ~Deuteronomy 31.6

Herod got pretty mad about the Magi not coming back to tell him where the baby could be found. It was a wonder he didn't bring the power of Rome's armies against them personally. Instead, he massacred children. Instead, he took it out on the people he ruled over attempting to wipe out any hope of a Savior for the people he ruled over.

His thirst for power and control was fueled by evil that seemed too dark to overcome. Yet, the light shone through.

It must have felt like a dark time for the Jews. Even with the rumors of the birth of their Messiah, it must have been hard to look past the hundreds of tiny caskets.

Still, the light shone through.

Psalm 139 says that God knew us in our mother's womb. God took all of those wee little ones to His side. The very children that evil men like Herod thought would bring on the destruction of God's people, were all taken home to be with Him. God won.

And, the light shone through.

Meanwhile, God had moved the Savior to another country. Once again, the plans of evil men would not triumph. Just as with Moses and Joseph and Esther, God ensured that His plan would move forward.

Considering all the darkness in the world, there is great comfort in that thought. God's character shines through even in these dark hours, even in the blackest of nights when it seems that evil is winning. The light will prevail and shine through.

God will always win. Joy will return.

He said so. I believe it.

Dear God, sometimes things seem pretty bleak. Sometimes the world's messiness and our feelings of fear and despair seem to consume us. We are thankful that you never leave, even when it *feels* like we are alone. Remind us to seek your face when we seem to be stumbling around in the darkness of today's world. Thanks for giving us that true, bright hope of your presence, no matter what. ~Amen

~~~~~~~

Waiting on Tiptoes
92

The Extraordinary Love of God

You can more easily catch a hurricane in a shrimp net than you can understand the wild, relentless, uncompromising, pursuing love of God presented at the manger. ~Brennan Manning

There is nothing ordinary, explainable, believable about the love of God. It surpasses all of our understanding that someone could love us with such grace and mercy. To absorb just a piece of it is an exercise of grandiose proportion.

God humbled himself, took on being a kid, disciplined by human parents (the ones He created), learned a trade (no calling on heavenly dad to bring a wooden bench magically into existence), allowed evil to drive stakes through His hands (the humans that he created and loved), and died (as a human, taking his last breath).

But He didn't stop there.

He came back to life and invited us to come to eternity with Him. He gave us the way. He loved completely, from the start in the stable to the empty tomb.

All so that we would see that life here on earth could be lived differently; that our lives could be more peaceful, more loving. All to turn us to Him—above all, in all, through all.

He showed us how to love by doing it. He showed us by walking on the very soil He had formed out of nothingness. He did it because He loves us so much that He could stand our disobedience not one second longer.

We couldn't figure it out ourselves. So He took us by the hand, sat us at his feet—his actual feet—and told us how to do it.

God became human.

It is so much more than we could ever imagine, so much more love than we could ever conjure up ourselves. He walked the walk, and He talked the talk, and died the death so that we could live.

Let ears hear. Let eyes see.

Dear Lord, it is hard to put into words, this love of yours. We cannot grasp it, not really. But we want to. Desperately, we want to show ourselves and the world what it looks like to love like you do. Help us and guide us in your ways, dear God. In your loving name, we pray for that. ~Amen

~~~~~~~

Waiting on Tiptoes
96

Seek God First

For God is greater than our hearts, and he knows everything. ~1 John 3.20

Love is a word thrown around these days as if we actually got it, that we actually lived out lives of real love. Oh, we certainly try to, we humans who think we've got it all together.

We know that God is love, that God wants us to love and be loved. So we say all the right words, in the right way. Our Facebook posts sometimes reflect a loving character, willingness to go the extra mile to love the unloveable (but all too often fall well short of that!).

The kind of love that God wants for us carries no social media braggadocia. To say I love like God does would mean that there is not a moment I let slip by that I don't love.

Here's the place where we all jump on the slippery slide into guilt and shame, the place where the Enemy loves to see us go. But that place is far from where God wants us.

We don't have to hang our head in shame because we don't love exactly like God does, that our love is not as sacrificial, as deep, as relentless. There is a simple reason for that.

We are NOT God. We just aren't. And will never be.

We are loved by a God who is so big and massive and incredible, that He understands our weak attempts at loving, at our mediocre displays of affection, at our often harsh words that could have been so much nicer.

And here's the catch of all catches. No matter how we struggle, how we fall down on this love-thing, we just need to keep seeking Him. In fact, we are to seek Him first.

When we do that, His love will start to flow out of us as He replaces our blackness with His purity. Seeking Him first, helps to make the annoying people not so annoying as we start to see them through His eyes, not ours alone.

The hard.to.loves will somehow become easier to reach out to.

Our character, our words, our whole being will be changed by His love. AS WE SEEK HIM.

Seek FIRST his kingdom... ~Matthew 6.33

Dear God, thanks so much for already being here in us. Forgive us for not seeking you more consistently than our haphazard emergency prayers, than our on-again-off-again devotionals. Help us to tap into your Spirit more often, every day. And by doing that, fill us with your love and grace that we can pour out all over anyone who crosses our paths. ~Amen

~~~~~~~

Waiting on Tiptoes
100

We Don't Have the Time

Heaven meets earth like an unforeseen kiss,
as my heart turns violently inside of my chest.
I don't have time to maintain these regrets,
when I think about the way he loves me...
~David Crowder, *He Loves Me*

Sometimes a song will grab me and not let go. The melody maybe, the words maybe, the crescendo in the chorus. But Crowder's song, *He Loves Me,* grabs me in all of those ways and more. Every time I hear it, my heart just smiles, then my eyes let loose with a few tears. Some music has that kind of effect on my soul.

I included my favorite verse from that song above, because there is one line from it that so often comes back to me at weird times, in odd places in my life. *I don't have time to maintain these regrets...*

Maintaining regrets.

I have spent a huge portion of my adult life in this maintenance mode. Maintaining emotions, fears, guilt, regrets that have no place in a life that boasts of Christ. Maintenance is exhausting because every time you enter its mode you must, for the sake of our twisted need for completeness, dig up all the crap that went along with it. Every emotion and all the faces, words and hurt.

When I think about the way he loves me... how can I possibly take the time to think about how much I don't love ME? Maintaining regrets leads us to a place of un-love, to these shameful niches in our life that scream that we are unworthy of this gift from God, of his love.

And we are wrong. Wrong to hold on to it. Wrong to keep the cycle of maintenance going. We just don't have the time. Instead, when we focus our energy on how much God loves us, it allows us to release the hold we have maintained on all the reasons God shouldn't love us.

Nothing will be able to separate us from the love of God. ~Romans 8.39

Dear God, we have few words to express what your love means to us. Help us to continue to absorb its mystery and fullness as we discard the regrets-maintenance mode in our lives. Forgive us for thinking less of ourselves, your creation, your love. Strengthen us as we throw out the old ways, the time wasters that have driven us away from you, rather than towards you. We love you, God. We love you. ~Amen

~~~~~~~

Waiting on Tiptoes
104

Love On Display

Whoever loves God should also love his brother. ~1 John 4.21

We all have a person or two in our lives that we consider to be hard to love. I know I do. When I try to show love to that un-loveable person, I am seized with this unjoyful gut-level feeling of guilt, of not "feeling" the love.

There is shame in having the non-feeling, in not wanting to even act on their behalf. How could I be a Christian and not *love* this person? It is a sick cycle of yuck.

It is simple to explain, taking any theological confusion out if it. The truth is that I just don't *like* that person. It really has nothing to do with loving her. But yet, aren't I supposed to show her love. Isn't love an action word?

Dallas Willard said that showing God's love means 'wanting the very best for the other person.'

I get what he meant. I don't believe I have one person in my life who I don't want the best for. But for some, I don't want to be the one giving it to 'em.

We too often strive to show love by doing what we really can't do. We try to do God's love the way the world defines it - doing certain things, in certain ways, that make you feel a certain emotion. If we don't, or can't, do it 'that' way, or 'feel' a certain way, then we are not loving like God.

A vicious spiral of guilt and shame and regret ensues, engulfing us in a joy-less role of benefactor of all love and kindness to a person we barely want to speak to. I do not believe that is what God meant when He said to love each other.

Showing God's love may not be a public display for all to see, for all to admire. Love may be silent and hidden, displayed in lots of ways that the world will never see, that the world will be unable to judge.

Be careful not to do your 'acts of right-eousness' before men, to be seen by them. If you do, you will have no reward from your Father in heaven. ~Matthew 6.1

How can you tell if you are loving like God? I am not all that sure. But I don't think it involves heart turmoil or fear or regrets or shame. I think it is peace and joy that engulfs you. And it's between you and God, empowered by Him, not by our own feeble efforts, or by the world's standards and rules and judgements.

Dear God, teach us to love like you do. Help us to love when we don't like. Help us to step back and rely on you to love through us when we cannot figure it out on our own. Thank you for loving us when we are unloveable, for being our all and all wherever we are. Teach us how to do that with each other. ~Amen

~~~~~~~

Waiting on Tiptoes
108

The Forever Gift

Freely you have received, freely give.
~Matthew 10.8

When I was in Kenya, working in the slums of Nairobi, I visited a classroom in the Christian school my church sponsors. To honor us the children sang. The words of their songs were always scripture verses. The one that has stuck with me over the years since I was there, is this one:

Even if my father and mother abandon me, the Lord will hold me close. ~Psalm 27.10 NLT

I didn't find that to be the most joyous choice for kids, right? The teacher told me they used this verse because they wanted the children, from first grade on, to not only know the words, but to understand its truth. I saw that as a nice sentiment, but these teachers of the poor see it as a necessity.

The majority of these kids have been abandoned by their parents—one or both. Sometimes it is because of death by AIDS. More often it is because of drug or alcohol addiction or the sheer hopelessness of abject poverty. For many kids, they are being raised by relatives or strangers who they may have never met before.

This verse gave these kids a firm foundation. They could rely on God's presence, even if mom and dad were gone. God was there. Always and forever.

This truth is not just for kids who live in poverty. It is for all of us.

I have been a Christian so long that sometimes I forget what it would be like to feel the aloneness of not having a God who is with me all the time. Even when fear and discouragement reign high, I always know deep in my heart that God will 'never leave me or forsake me.' (Deuteronomy 31.6,8)

What would being alone, really alone, in the world be like? How would a worldview that has no eternal solution change how we live? Where would evil lead if no One is in control, if no One is there to work it all out in the end? No hope to lean on. No Holy Spirit to comfort. Just the fallen world destroying itself.

Christmas is not just about a baby in a manger. Christmas is about the birth of our forever-comforter, our go-to hope in time of need. Christmas is about the incredible gift of non-aloneness.

Jesus said, I will ask the Father and he will GIVE you another Counselor to be with you forever. ~John 14.16

What a joyous, too-often-taken-for-granted, forever gift.

Dear God, thank you for your gift of You. Forgive us for taking it for granted all too often, for not choosing to be grateful for it more often. Forgive us for putting it away on the shelf with the other decorations, to bring out again next year. Show us, Lord, through your Spirit how to shower our world with your gift, all year long. ~Amen

~~~~~~~~

God is Near

The grace of God means something like:
Here is your life. You might never have been,
but you are, because the party wouldn't have
been complete without you. Here is the world.
Beautiful and terrible things will happen.
Don't be afraid. I am with you. ~Frederick
Buechner

Imagine a night of thunder and lightening. The electricity in the air crackles close to your shelter. Your imagination runs wild. What if the lightening hits the roof? What if the house catches on fire? What if it hits the tree and the tree falls on the house? What if... What if... is the phrase that begins almost every fear spiral. Anxiety fills your being. The storm seems to be endless.

Then your dad walks in. Maybe not really your actual dad but the dad you always wanted. The one that comes between you and your fears, the one who puts anxiety out of business. Maybe you have an earthly dad like that, maybe not. But imagine for a minute that he, smelling of bacon and sawdust, engulfs you in his arms clad with the soft fleece jacket that is always so warm and comforting. Imagine that, muffled into his arms, you can no longer see the flashes of lightening, the thunder almost neutralized by his gentle rocking.

Imagine that.

That's as close as I can come to envisioning God being near. A small piece, a fuzzy glimpse. The Bible says that God 'knows the way to where the lightening is dispersed. He cuts a channel for the torrents of rain, and a path for the thunderstorms.' He holds the storms in His hands. They are nothing to Him. He can control all of that. Somehow. Some way.

There is no way to understand that, to really grasp it. We need only accept that God is greater than we can possibly know.

When we fear, God is as near as a word, as close as my fingertip reaching out, as willing as my lungs are to breath in. He is with us, and in us, and all around us, all at the same time.

The amazing, wondrous, miracle of Christmas.

He is Christmas and the Resurrection. He is my personal God and He is the God of the Universe.

He is the wonder of the baby and I am safe with Him.

Dear God, thank you for being the God that we understand, and the God that we don't. Thank you for being bigger and more powerful and more awesome than our human brains will ever grasp. Thank you for your gift of being near, and engulfing us in your protection. And thank you for being with us always and forever. Thank you. ~Amen

~~~~~~~~

Waiting on Tiptoes
116

Forever in the Light

"Yes, I am coming soon!" Amen. Come, Lord Jesus. ~Revelation 22.20

To all: a prayer for a joyous, hope-filled, peace-drenched holiday of love for each other, for yourself, and for the God who became real in a manger so we can be free.

Dear Lord,

Thank you for Christmas, for what you did that we celebrate.

By the manger, Mary pondered it.

By the shining skies, the shepherds heard of it.

By the star, the Magi followed it.

In the Old Testament you said you will come. You did.

In the New Testament you said you will be back. You will.

Until then, we are not alone.

Until then, you are our Spirit, our comforter, our guide.

Until then, we will endure.

We will have joy, we will weep, and we will laugh.

We will have your peace always at our call.

You will return. Then we will no longer ponder.

Then we will hear, and we will see.

And we will forever live in your light.

~Amen

Waiting on Tiptoes
119

Waiting on Tiptoes
120

www.ingramcontent.com/pod-product-compliance
Lightning Source LLC
Chambersburg PA
CBHW020550030426
42337CB00013B/1033